I0450414

United States
Department of
Agriculture

Forest Service

Pacific Northwest
Research Station

General Technical Report
PNW-GTR-861

May 2012

The Asian Wood Pellet Markets

Joseph A. Roos and Allen M. Brackley

Authors

Joseph A. Roos is a researcher at the University of Washington, College of the Environment, Box 352100, Seattle, WA 98195; and **Allen M. Brackley** is a research forester, U.S. Department of Agriculture, Forest Service, Pacific Northwest Research Station, Alaska Wood Utilization Research and Development Center, 204 Siginaka Way, Sitka, AK 99835.

Cover photographs: Scenes from Superior Wood Pellet plant in North Pole, Alaska. Clockwise from upper left: pelleting machine; pellets bagged for home use; a Superior Pellet Fuels bag; inventory of product ready for shipment to retailers. Upper right photo by David Nicholls; all others by Allen M. Brackley.

Abstract

Roos, Joseph A.; Brackley, Allen, M. 2012. The Asian Wood Pellet Markets. Gen Tech Rep. PNW-GTR-861. Portland, OR. U.S. Department of Agriculture, Forest Service, Pacific Northwest Research Station. 25 p.

This study examines the three major wood pellet markets in Asia: China, Japan, and South Korea. In contrast to the United States, where most wood pellets are used for residential heating with pellet stoves, a majority of the wood pellets in Asia are used for co-firing at coal-fired power plants. Our analysis indicated that Japan is the largest importer of wood pellets in Asia and that most of the pellets it consumes are used for co-firing at power plants. South Korean wood pellet imports are fairly small; however, South Korea is striving to increase its percentage of renewable energy, which could benefit the wood pellets industry. We found that China, the largest energy consumer in Asia, has an established wood pellet market. However, a majority of these wood pellets are manufactured in China, thus imports are minimal. A consistent factor in these nations is that their governments are promoting renewable energy, leading to policies that are driving demand for wood pellets. As these countries strive to meet their renewable energy targets, their wood pellet consumption is projected to grow.

Keywords: Renewable energy, wood pellets, Asia, China, Japan, South Korea.

Contents

Introduction

Global wood pellet production was approximately 12 million metric tons in 2009, and is predicted to increase to 100 million metric tons by 2020 (Bloomberg 2010a). The primary drivers for increasing global demand for wood pellets are government policies and global agreements in support of renewable sources of energy. The first major climate-change agreement to reduce greenhouse gas (GHG) emissions was the Kyoto Protocol, developed under the United Nations Framework Convention on Climate Change (UNFCCC). The Kyoto Protocol went into effect in February 2005 and set a target for reducing GHG emissions by signatory countries to an average of 5 percent below 1990 levels between 2008 and 2012. The UNFCCC is now planning for a new climate-change agreement to follow the Kyoto Protocol. Representatives from various countries met in Copenhagen in December 2009 to discuss a post-Kyoto Protocol climate-change agreement. Although no concrete agreement emerged, the meeting produced a draft that stipulates that global emissions be reduced "to hold the increase in global temperature below 2 degrees Celsius, and take action to meet this objective consistent with science and on the basis of equity" (UNFCCC 2010).

Although the United States did not participate in the Kyoto Protocol, there is movement in the United States to reduce GHG emissions. On April 17, 2009, the U.S. Environmental Protection Agency (EPA) formally announced its determination that GHGs pose a threat to public health and the environment (EPA 2009). This announcement was significant because it gives the executive branch the authority to impose carbon regulations on carbon-emitting entities. There are also two major climate change bills that have been introduced by the legislative branch. The first is The American Clean Energy and Security Act, also known as the Waxman-Markey Bill, in the House. The second is the American Power Act, also known as the Kerry-Lieberman Bill, in the Senate. The Waxman-Markey bill calls for a 20-percent reduction of greenhouse gas emissions from 2005 levels by 2020, and the Kerry-Lieberman bill calls for a 17-percent reduction over the same period. The Waxman-Markey bill also sets a mandate for renewable energy, requiring 25 percent of all energy sold to be sourced from renewable energy by 2025. However, as of this writing (August 2010), both of these bills appear to be temporarily shelved in favor of an energy bill proposed in 2010 by Senate Majority Leader Harry Reid.

While the energy policy in the United States remains unclear, Japan and South Korea have established renewable energy policies that are increasing demand for wood pellets. The purpose of this paper is to examine the Asian wood pellet market and the potential for U.S. wood pellet exports.

The Global Energy Portfolio

By 2035, global energy consumption is projected to increase approximately 50 percent from current levels (EIA 2010). The top three global energy sources are oil, coal, and natural gas; and these three sources supply approximately 86 percent of the world's energy, requirements (fig. 1). There are many types of renewable energy including hydroelectric, geothermal, wind, solar, tidal and wave, and biomass energy. Although oil, coal, and natural gas are expected to remain the world's primary sources of energy, renewable energy, including hydroelectric power, is projected to increase to 100 quadrillion British Thermal Units (BTU), or 14 percent of global energy consumption, by 2035 (fig. 2).

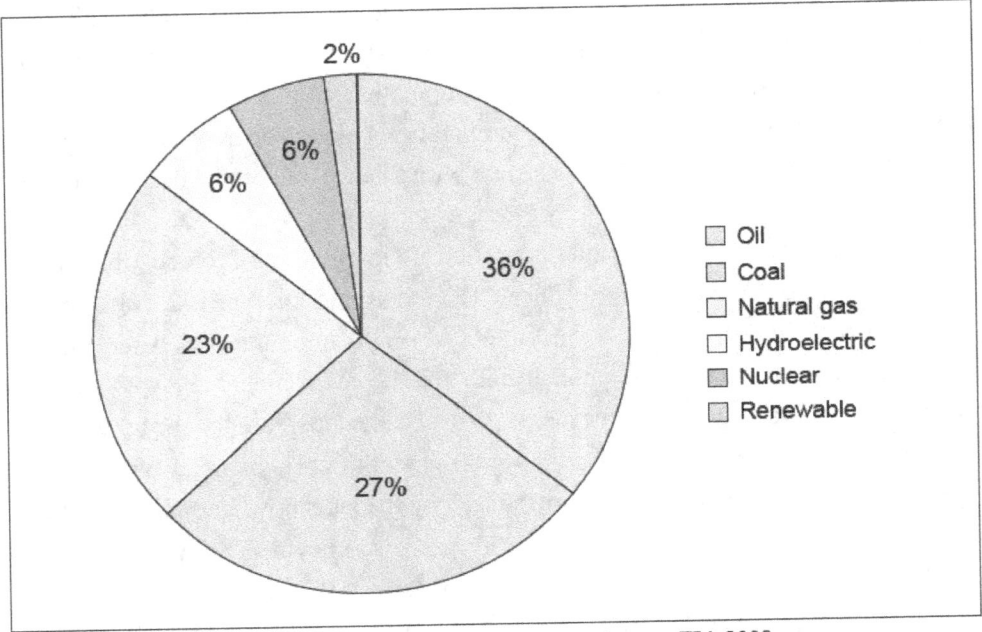

Figure 1—Percentage of global energy production by source. Source: EIA 2008.

Biomass Energy

Biomass energy refers to energy stored in organic material such as forest and agricultural products. Biomass is a key energy source in the developing world in the form of firewood used for heating and cooking. In the developed world, biomass energy is gaining popularity as a fuel source for electricity generation. One advantage that biomass has over wind and solar power is that it can generate electricity continuously or on a schedule, rather than relying on conditions of the wind or sun. The primary feedstock of biomass for heat and electricity generation is woody biomass. Other sources include corn, soy, crop residues, and grasses. Global production of biomass, waste, and ocean-based sources of energy is predicted to

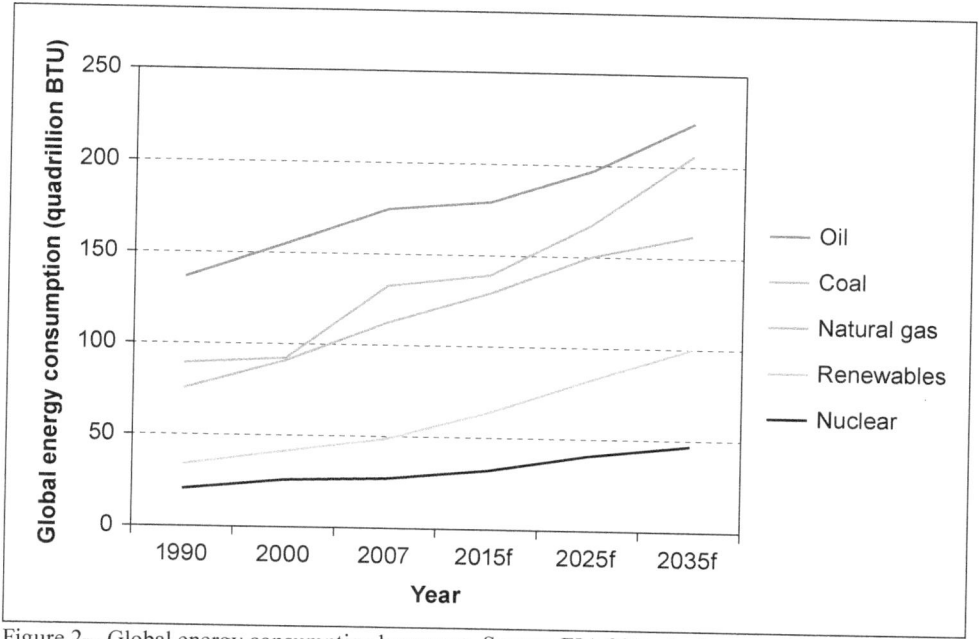

Figure 2—Global energy consumption by source. Source: EIA 2010; f = forecast; BTU=British thermal units.

increase more than three times the 2007 level by 2035 (fig. 3). There are various methods to generate heat and electricity using biomass feedstocks (Pew Center for Global Climate Change 2009):

- Direct firing—Biomass is the only fuel used at a given power plant. The feedstock is fed into a boiler, which in turn powers a steam turbine to generate electricity. The direct firing method attains efficiencies of up to 40 percent.

- Co-firing—Biomass is substituted for a portion of the coal burned in a coal-fired power plant. A coal-fired power plant can be modified to accommodate biomass and use it to supply up to 20 percent of its fuel requirements. This method reaches efficiencies between 33 and 37 percent.

- Cogeneration—Fuel is burned to produce both electricity and heat. As with direct firing, the biomass fuel powers a steam turbine generator. However, unlike direct firing, cogeneration uses the resulting exhaust flow for further electricity generation or heat generation. The advantage of cogeneration is improved efficiencies between 75 and 90 percent.

- Gasification—Feedstock is processed in a hot oxygen-starved area to produce a gas, composed mostly of carbon monoxide and hydrogen. This gas fuels a turbine to produce electricity. This method reaches efficiencies of up to 60 percent.

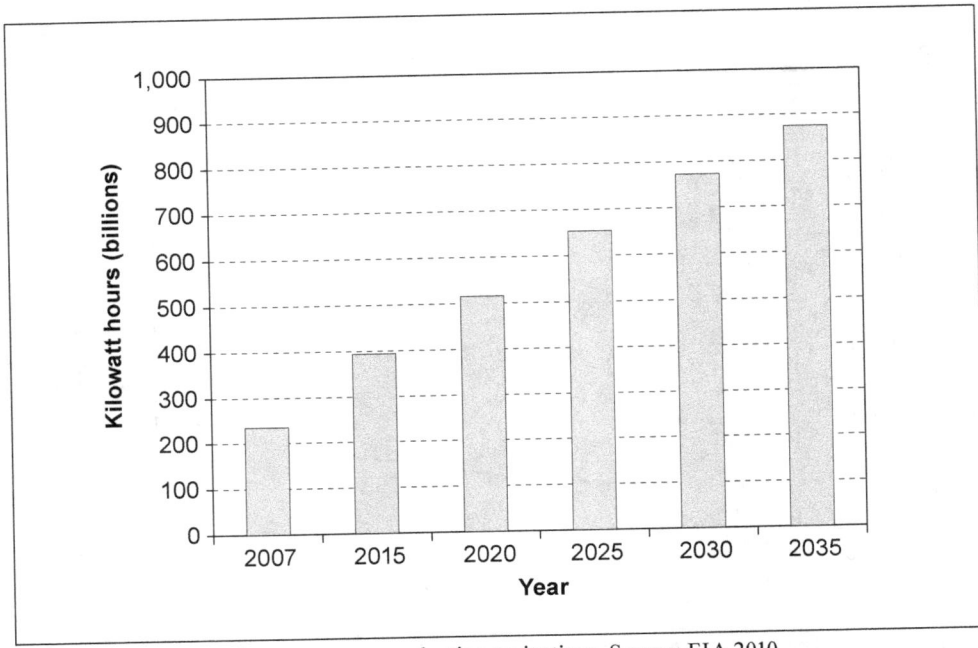

Figure 3—Biomass and ocean energy production projections. Source: EIA 2010.

Wood Pellets

Wood pellets are one type of biomass energy. Pellets are primarily manufactured from wood waste, including sawdust, shavings, and wood chips, which are byproducts of the manufacture of lumber, furniture, and other forest products. The pellet manufacturing process consists of the following steps: receipt of raw materials, screening, grinding, drying, pelletizing, cooling, screening, and packaging. The raw materials should be dried to the desired moisture content (Brackley and Parrent 2011, Hansen et al. 2009). Once the material is dried, it is ground so that each piece has a diameter that meets proper specifications. In some cases, the raw material is then conditioned in a steam conditioner to soften the wood before it is compacted. This makes the raw material less abrasive to the equipment. The next step is the pelletizing itself. Pellet machines apply pressure to force the raw materials through holes that shape the pellets. Pressure and friction are used to increase the temperature of the wood, which in turn allows the lignum to soften and the wood fibers to be reshaped into pellets. After the pellets leave the extruder, they are air-cooled, the lignums solidify, and the pellet is formed. The dimensions, density, and other factors are specified by standards designed by industry groups. In the United States, the Pellet Fuel Institute has designed a set of standards for wood pellet fuel grading (table 1).

Table 1—Pellet Fuels Institute standards, effective October 27, 2010 (PFI 2010)

Fuel property	Premium grade	Standard grade	Utility grade
Bulk density	40.0–46.0	38.0–46.0	38.0–46.0
Diameter (inches)	0.230–0.285	0.230–0.285	0.230–0.285
Diameter (mm)	5.84–7.25	5.84–7.25	5.84–7.25
Pellet durability index	≥96.5	≥95.0	≥95.0
Fines (percent at mill gate)	≤1.0	≤1.00	≤1.00
Inorganic ash percentage	≤1.0	≤2.00	≤6.0
Length (percentage > 1.5 inches)	≤1.0	≤1.0	≤1.0
Moisture percentage (wet basis)	≤6.0	≤10.0	≤10.0
Chloride (parts per million)	≤300	≤300	≤300

Global Wood Pellet Market Overview

The global economy is gradually recovering from the worst economic downturn since the Great Depression. The World Bank predicted that global gross domestic product (GDP) growth for 2010 would be 3.3 percent, which is double the 2008 level (World Bank 2010). This new phase of global expansion will stimulate demand for more energy, including wood pellets.

The major wood pellet-producing countries in North America and Europe are Canada, Germany, Sweden, and the United States. The major consumer countries for wood pellets are Belgium, Denmark, the Netherlands, Sweden, and the United States (fig. 4). The major wood pellet importing countries are Belgium, Denmark, the Netherlands, and Sweden. As figure 4 shows, the United States produces a large quantity of wood pellets but also consumes a large quantity. In contrast, Canada produces a large quantity of wood pellets but exports approximately 80 percent of its production.

The European wood pellet market can be divided into two segments: electric power generation and heating. Denmark, Finland, and Sweden use wood pellets for both heating and electricity generation. In contrast, Austria, France, Germany, and Italy use pellets mostly for heating (Peksa-Blanchar et al. 2007).

The European wood pellet industry can be traced back to Sweden in the late 1970s, when equipment was developed for converting oil boilers to pellet fuel use. Stimulation of a viable wood-pellet industry increased in the 1990s, starting in 1991 when the Swedish government implemented a tax on fossil fuels. As Belgium, Denmark, Germany and the Netherlands adopted similar policies, the European wood pellet market began to expand rapidly.

A large part of European wood pellet demand can be attributed to the Kyoto Protocol requirement to reduce GHG emissions 5 percent below 1990 levels. Many European coal-fired power plants have found that co-firing with biomass energy is a cost-effective way to reduce GHG emissions. Another key policy that increased

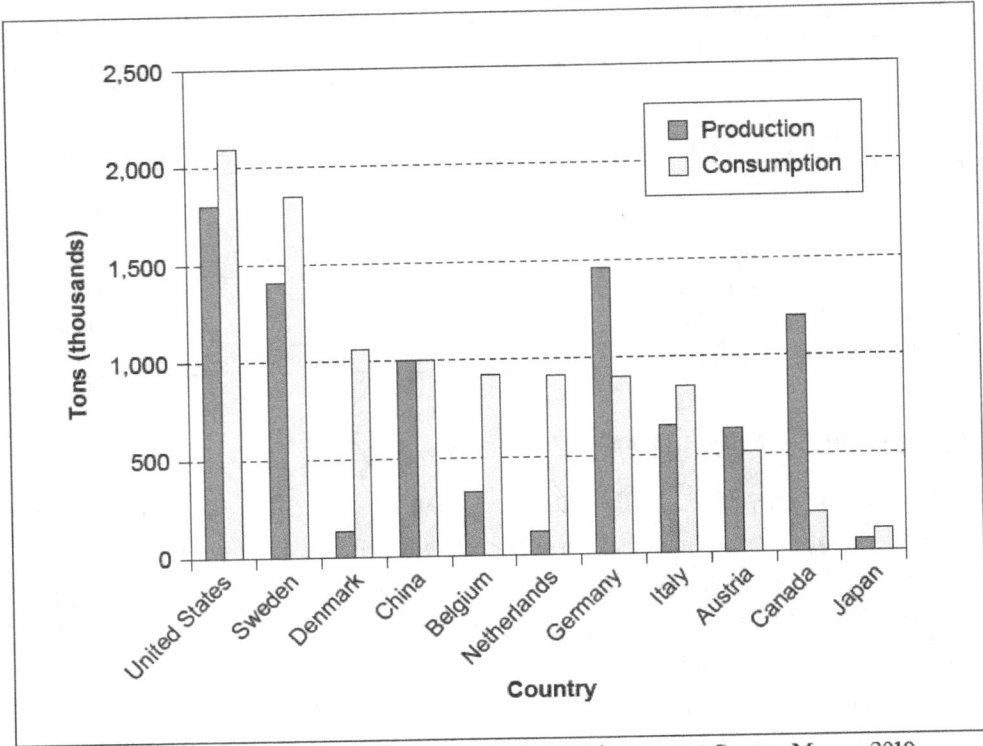

Figure 4—Wood pellet production and consumption in 2009 by country. Source: Murray 2010.

wood pellet demand in Europe was the European Biomass Action Plan of 2005. The European Union (EU) generated approximately 4 percent of its 2005 energy needs from biomass energy. The goal of the European Biomass Action Plan was to promote research and development and increase utilization of biomass energy. This plan also set a target of increasing biomass energy to 8 percent of total energy production by 2010, a goal that has increased demand for wood pellets.

The North American market for wood pellets began to gain traction in the late 1970s. Initially, wood pellets were used mainly by industrial, commercial, and institutional sectors for heating. Then pellets began to enter the residential heating market as pellet-fueled heating stoves gained popularity. Currently, the United States provides a federal tax credit for renewable energy generation, the Renewable Energy Production Tax Credit, which provides a 2.2 cent-per-kilowatt-hour (kWh) tax credit for wind, geothermal, and closed-loop biomass energy production (DSIRE 2010). There are also various incentives in support of renewable energy at the state, county, and local government levels.

Wood pellet production in 2010 was estimated to be 1.8 million metric tons in the United States and 1.2 million metric tons in Canada (Murray 2010). Most of the U.S. pellet production was consumed domestically, with only 20 percent of total production exported. The primary wood pellet use in the United States is home heating in pellet stoves, thus most of the production is packaged in 40-pound (18-kilogram) bags (Spelter and Toth 2009). In contrast to the United States, 83 percent of Canadian 2009 production was exported and shipped in bulk.

Researchers have also examined the potential for biomass energy to meet Alaska's heating and energy needs. Forests cover 129 million acres of Alaska, or about one third of the state; given this vast resource, wood energy has the potential to supply a significant portion of Alaska's energy demands. Currently, wood energy is being used to heat residences, schools, community centers, and commercial buildings. Nicholls (2009) examined the potential role of wood in providing energy to Alaska's rural communities. This study found that the main limitations of wood energy include the availability of woody biomass, fuel moisture content, and transportation costs. The research also found that, in certain cases, wood burners worked well to meet the heating needs of rural communities. An analysis of the Kenai Peninsula showed that the payback period ranged from 4 to 20 years depending on competing fuel, machinery, and other factors (Nicholls and Crimp 2002).

Wood pellet market research is a fairly new field, with most of the studies focusing on the North American and European markets. However, while these markets are well established, a number of Asian governments are developing policies to promote the use of renewable energy, and wood pellets are benefitting from these policies. The following section examines Asian markets for wood pellets and their potential as markets for U.S. exports.

Asian Wood Pellet Markets

The Asian wood pellet market is expanding at a steady pace. This can be seen in the quantity of wood pellet exports from the Port of Prince Rupert, British Columbia, to Asia, which increased 33 percent in the first half of 2010 over the same period in the previous year (Prince Rupert Port Authority 2010). The west coast is in a strong position to supply Asia with wood pellets, drawing on both timber supply and proximity to Asian markets.

Most of the wood pellets shipped to Asia are directed to two markets. The first is the industrial energy sector, where pellets are used for co-firing with coal at power plants and in large boilers. The second is the home heating market, where pellets are used in pellet stoves. Generally, wood pellets shipped to the industrial energy markets in Asia are shipped via bulk carrier rather than by container ships. The three largest consumers of wood pellets in Asia are China, South Korea, and Japan; the following sections provide an overview of their general economies, energy needs, and wood pellet markets.

China's Wood Pellet Market

China's 2008 GDP was US$4.3 trillion. Although the world's GDP growth contracted 2 percent in 2009, China's GDP growth surged at 8.7 percent (fig. 5). Much of this growth was fueled by infrastructure projects funded by government stimulus funds. China's GDP growth was projected to be between 9 percent and 10 percent in 2010, then to slow to 8.3 percent in 2011 (EIU 2010).

One area of contention between China and its trading partners has been the manipulation of the Chinese currency to keep it at artificially undervalued levels. This practice has kept the price of goods exported from China low, while keeping the price of goods imported into China high. However, on June 19, 2010, the Chinese government announced it would be more flexible in managing its currency. As a result, the Chinese yuan appreciated against the U.S. dollar for the first time since July 2005, making U.S. exports somewhat cheaper for Chinese consumers (Bloomberg 2010b).

China is currently the second largest consumer of energy in the world, behind the United States. Energy has been the foundation of China's economic growth. At the center of China's energy consumption is coal, which provides China with 70 percent of its energy needs, making it the world's largest coal consumer. Oil

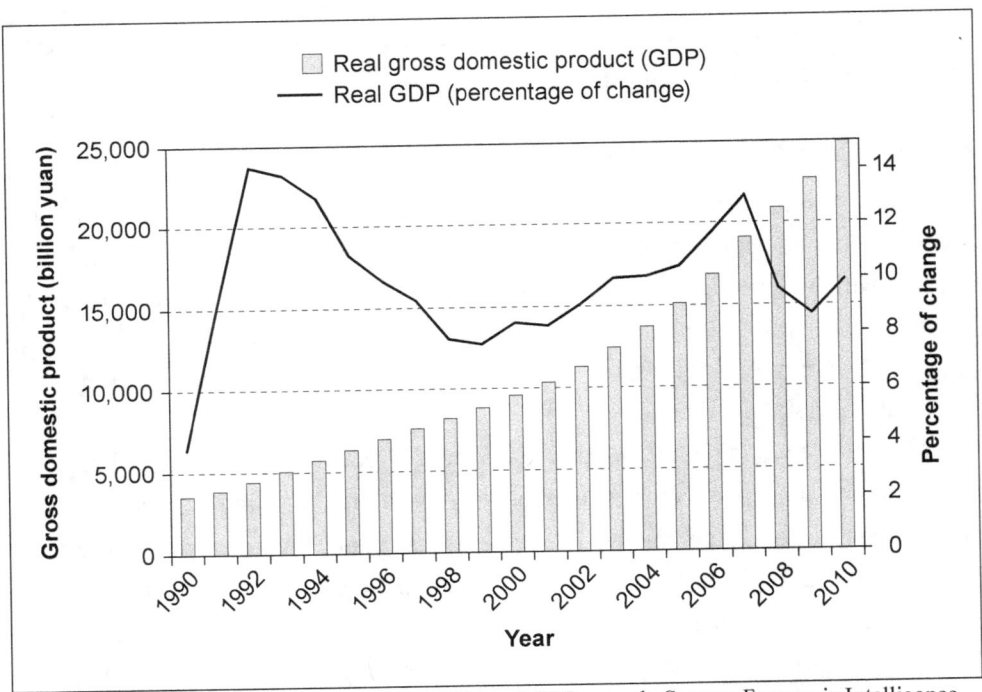

Figure 5—China's gross domestic product (GDP) and GDP growth. Source: Economic Intelligence Unit 2010.

accounts for approximately 20 percent of China's energy consumption and the remaining 10 percent comes from natural gas, renewable energy, and nuclear energy (fig. 6).

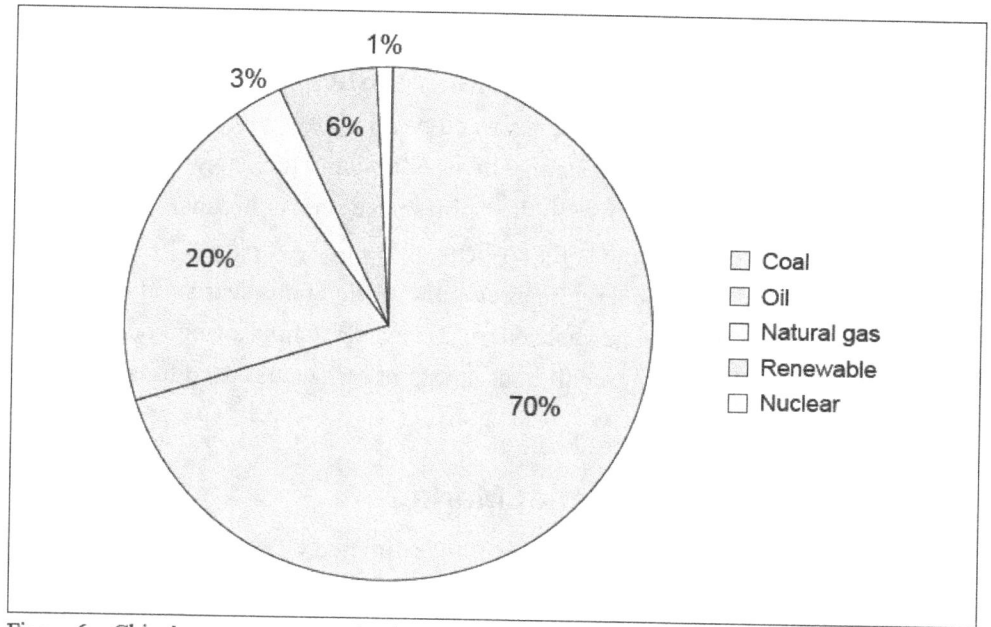

Figure 6—China's energy consumption by type. Source: Economic Intelligence Unit 2009.

China's energy policy is to secure enough energy to fuel its continued economic growth. China has been hesitant to commit to any global climate-change agreement that mandates emission reductions. Its official position on climate change is the "principle of common but differentiated responsibilities" (National Development and Reform Commission 2009). This policy takes the position that developed countries need to take responsibility for their historical cumulative emissions and their current high per capita emissions. China has agreed to pursue the common goal of mitigating the impacts of climate change but has resisted committing to any specific emission-reduction goals.

Although China has avoided committing to mandatory emission reductions, it is investing heavily in renewable energy. The basis for China's renewable energy policy is its Renewable Energy Law, which was enacted January 1, 2006. This law mandates that power grid companies purchase all the renewable energy that can be supplied to their grids. An amendment to this law was enacted on April 1, 2010, that increases the enforcement of the mandatory purchase clause and increases support for the purchase of renewable energy (Schaub 2010). China also has mandated that at least 15 percent of their its capacity be generated from renewable energy sources by 2015 (China Daily 2009).

Biomass fuel development is a top priority in China. One area China is examining to supplement its coal use is wood pellets (Wang 2005). China's production of wood pellets was estimated to be 800 000 metric tons in 2008 (Swaan 2008) and 1 million metric tons in 2009 (Yamamoto et al. 2009). China's wood pellet consumption relies primarily on domestic production, and imports are minimal. In 2008, China imported approximately US$10.3 million dollars of wood fuel; only a fraction of this figure was for wood pellets (FAO 2010). However, the Chinese currency has appreciated against the U.S. dollar, which may make U.S. wood pellets more cost-competitive in the Chinese market. As in Japan, the major market for wood pellets in China is for co-firing at coal power plants. In summary, China has the second largest energy market in the world and is searching for ways to increase its percentage of renewable energy. However, China's wood pellet import volume is still relatively small, thus strong efforts would need to be made in market development.

South Korea's Wood Pellet Market

South Korea has a strong economy with a 2009 estimated GDP of US$1.36 trillion (fig. 7). As with many other global economies, South Korea's 2009 economic growth was sluggish at 0.2 percent. However, the Bank of Korea forecast its 2010 GDP to grow at a rate of 5.2 percent. The South Korean government reacted swiftly and effectively to the global economic crisis, while maintaining sound fiscal policies. Additionally, South Korea's exports have been strong and the country is gaining market share on its Japanese rivals in key markets such as electronics and automobiles. As a result of its strong fundamentals, South Korea's credit rating was upgraded by Moody's Investor Service in April 2010 (Bloomberg 2010c).

South Korea's steady economic growth has been fueled by fossil fuel energy, which has sharply increased carbon dioxide (CO_2) emissions. From 1990 to 2006, South Korea's CO_2 output increased by approximately 97 percent. This is in sharp contrast to neighboring Japan, which increased by 11 percent during the same period (United Nations Statistics Division 2010). The top three energy sources for South Korea are oil, coal, and natural gas, respectively (fig. 8). Although oil is the largest energy source, South Korea has substantially reduced its reliance on oil. Currently, South Korea's oil consumption is approximately 35 percent of total energy consumption, a substantial decrease from the 65-percent level of 1994 (EIA 2010). As oil consumption has been decreasing, nuclear power and natural gas have been increasing.

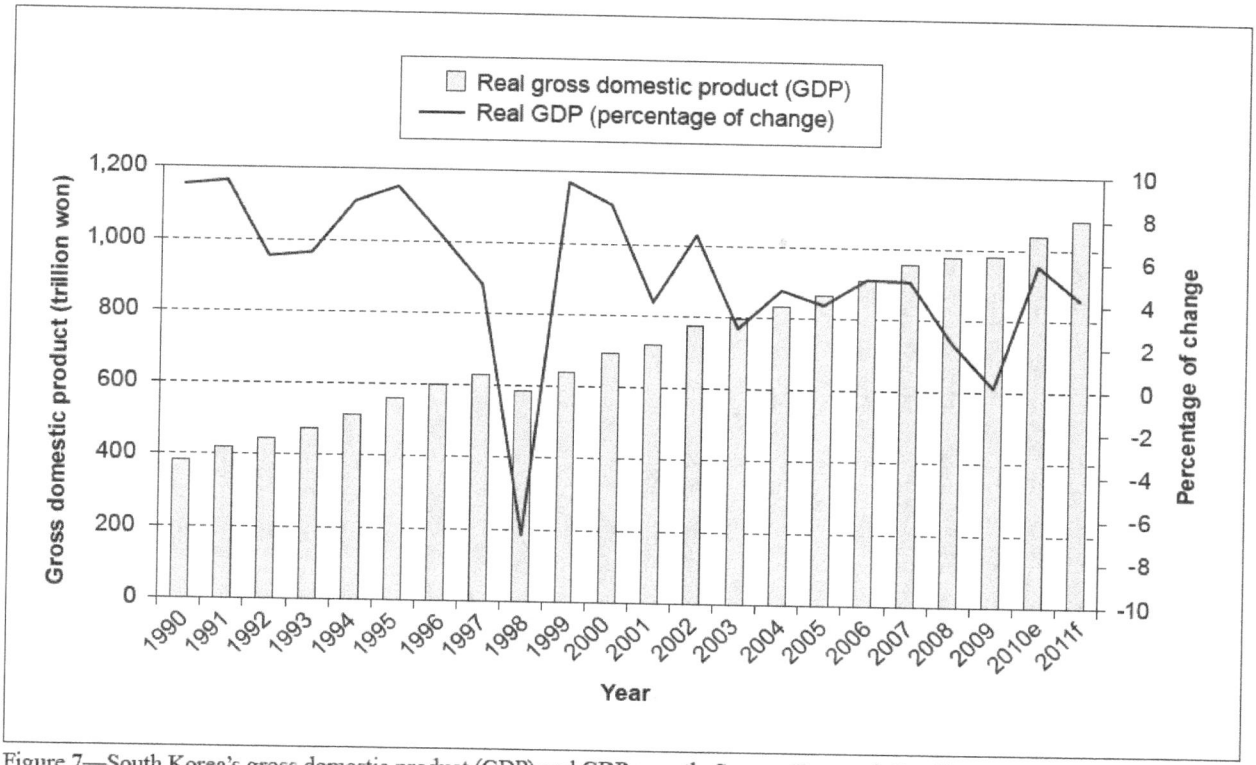

Figure 7—South Korea's gross domestic product (GDP) and GDP growth. Source: Economic Intelligence Unit 2010; e=estimate; f=forecast.

South Korea is taking aggressive steps to increase its renewable energy resources, including wind power, tidal power, and biofuels. Under President Lee Myung Bak, the country has pursued an energy policy that aims for energy security, economic efficiency, and environmental protection. This policy calls for the reduction of fossil fuels from the 2007 level of 83 percent of total energy use to 61 percent, and aims to increase renewable energy from the 2007 level of 2.4 percent to 11 percent by 2030 (IEA 2008).

South Korea relies heavily on imports for forest products, with a forest products self-sufficiency rate of only 6 percent (Korea Forest Service 2010). The top three exporters of forest products to South Korea are China, Malaysia, and New Zealand (Global Trade Atlas 2010). Wood energy development is being promoted by the Korea Forest Service. One unique approach South Korea is taking is to jointly develop wood energy technology and resources with other countries. In March 2009, the Korea Forest Service and the Indonesia Forest Ministry signed a pact to put aside 200 000 ha of forest land in Indonesia to produce wood pellets starting in 2010 (Thai Indian News 2009).

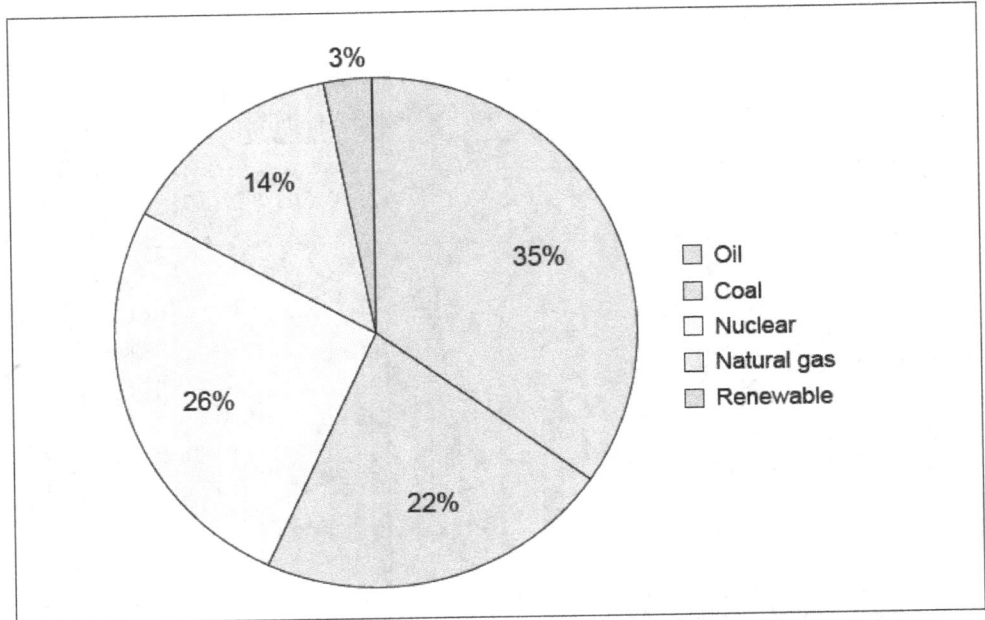

Figure 8—South Korea's energy consumption by type. Source: Economic Intelligence Unit 2009.

In 2009, South Korea's total pellet market was estimated to be 30 000 metric tons, with 10 000 metric tons being imported and 20 000 metric tons being produced domestically (Han 2009). Wood pellet demand was projected to more than double by 2012 to 750 000 metric tons, then increase to 5 million metric tons by 2020 (fig. 9).

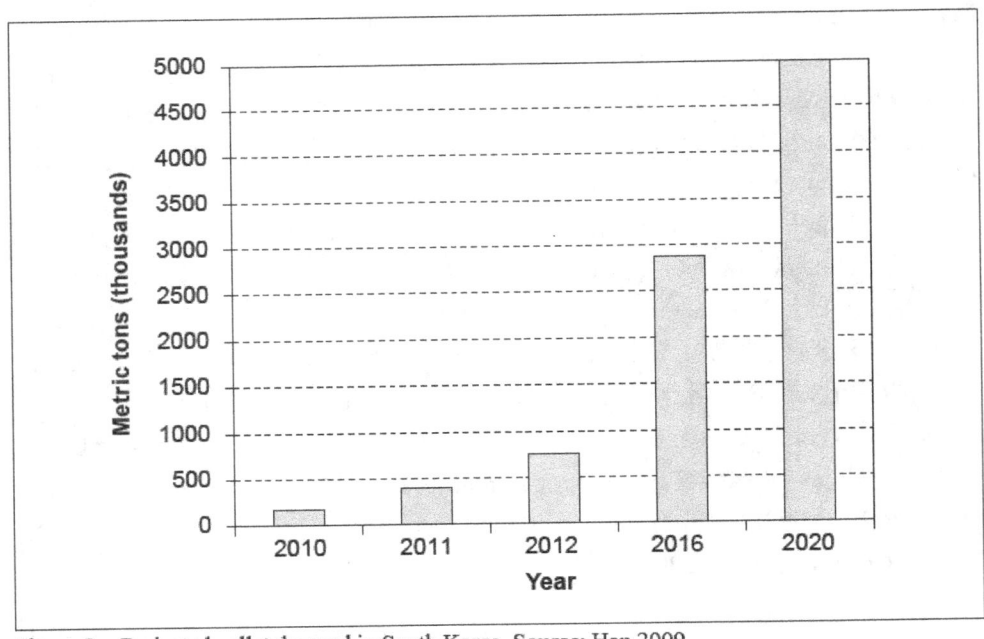

Figure 9—Projected pellet demand in South Korea. Source: Han 2009.

These projections are based on South Korea increasing its portion of renewable energy in order to meet the 11 percent renewable energy requirement by 2020. This 2020 requirement, combined with firm economic growth, makes South Korea a strong wood pellet market. However, currently its import quantity is fairly low, so U.S. exporters would need to establish relationships and invest in business development.

Japan's Wood Pellet Market

Japan's 2009 GDP was approximately US$4.14 trillion. After the collapse of the nation's real estate bubble in 1990, the Japanese economy entered what is known as the "lost decade," which describes Japan's stagnant economy between 1991 and 2001, when GDP growth rates averaged 1.2 percent annually and the government struggled to stimulate the economy (fig. 10). The global economic recession of 2008 hit Japan harder than China and South Korea. In 2009, Japan's economy contracted by 5.2 percent from the previous year. In contrast, the South Korean economy held its ground and China grew by 8.7 percent. One problem that continues to plague Japan is its government debt. Japan's efforts to stimulate its economy through infrastructure projects during the last 20 years has left the government saddled with a debt load that is almost twice the country's GDP (Bloomberg 2010d). In June 2010, Japan's parliament installed a new prime minister, Naoto Kan, who said he would make reducing the debt a top priority and that he may raise the national sales

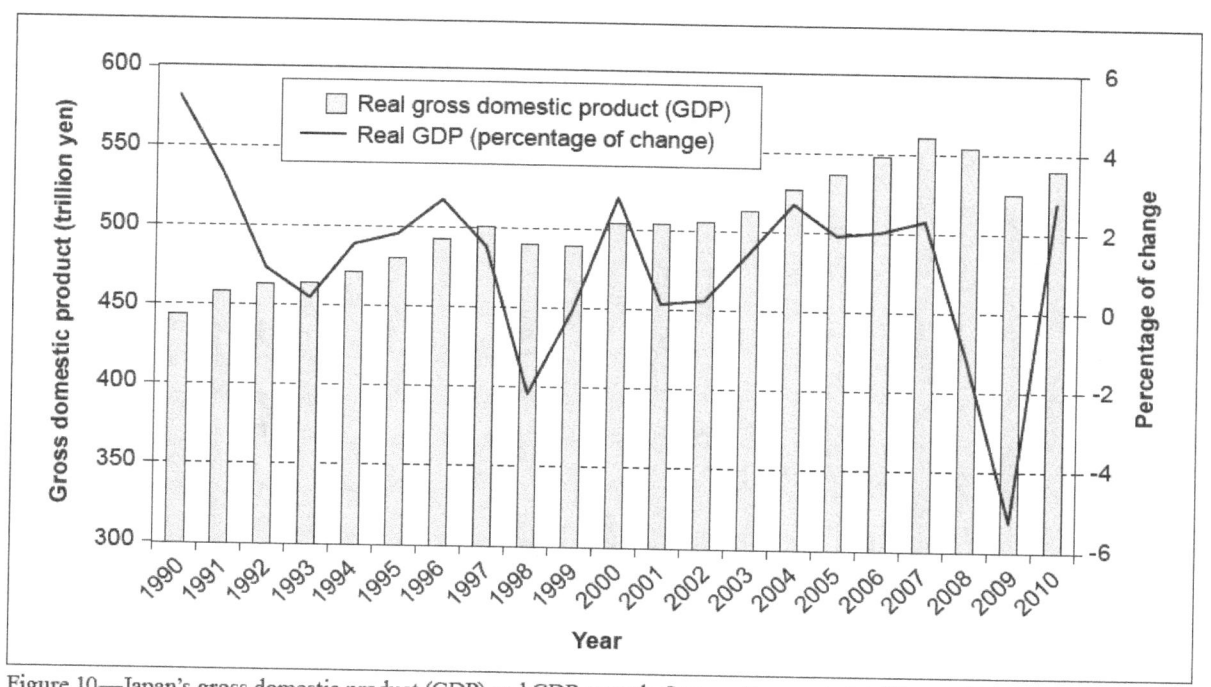

Figure 10—Japan's gross domestic product (GDP) and GDP growth. Source: Economic Intelligence Unit 2010.

tax. However, if the new administration increases the national sales tax, this could further hinder Japan's economic recovery.

Japan has almost no natural resources, so it imports almost all of its coal, oil, and natural gas supplies. Japan is the world's largest importer of natural gas and second largest importer of oil. The top three sources of Japan's energy consumption are oil at 49 percent, coal at 20 percent, and natural gas at 14 percent (fig. 11). The remaining energy consumption is made up of hydroelectric, nuclear, and non-hydro renewable sources. Japan is a signatory member of the Kyoto Protocol agreement and is required to reduce emissions by 6 percent below 1990 levels by 2012. To meet these targets, Japan was striving to increase its supply of nuclear and renewable energy. The center of this effort is Japan's Renewable Energy Portfolio Standard Law, which was enacted on April 1, 2003. This law sets the target to increase renewable energy to 16 billion kilowatt hours by 2014 (IEA 2007). This figure is double the amount of 2005 renewable energy generated in Japan. The types of renewable energy stipulated in the law are solar, wind, biomass, hydroelectric, and geothermal power.

The wood pellet industry is firmly established in Japan and is used for home heating as well as for power generation. In 2003, Japan produced an estimated 2400 metric tons of wood pellets, which increased to 60000 metric tons by 2008 (fig. 12). The Japan Wood Pellet Association reports that there are 55 wood pellet manufacturing facilities in Japan (Japan Wood Pellet Association 2010).

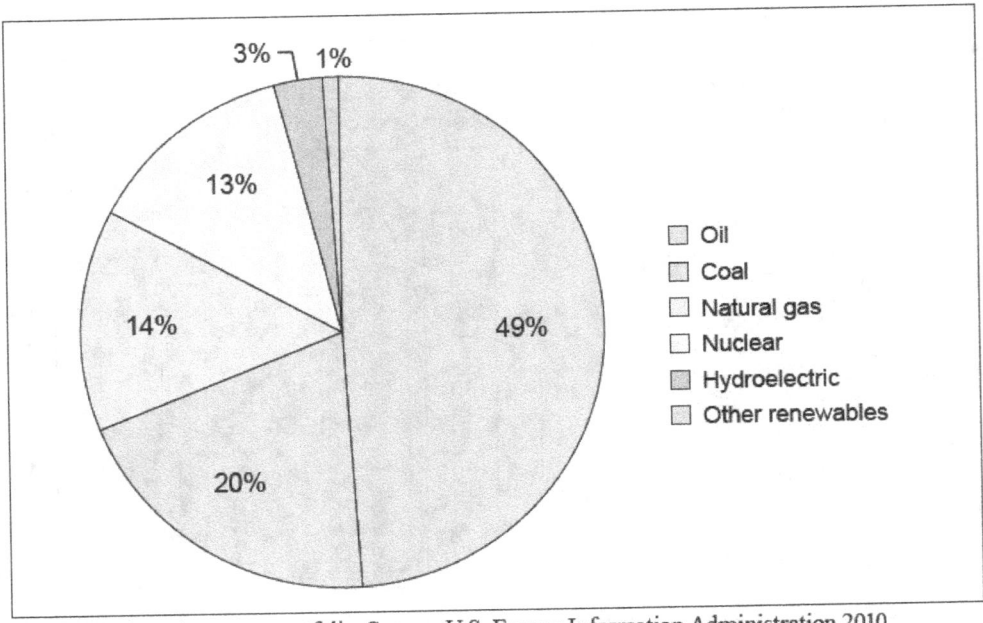

Figure 11—Japan's energy portfolio. Source: U.S. Energy Information Administration 2010.

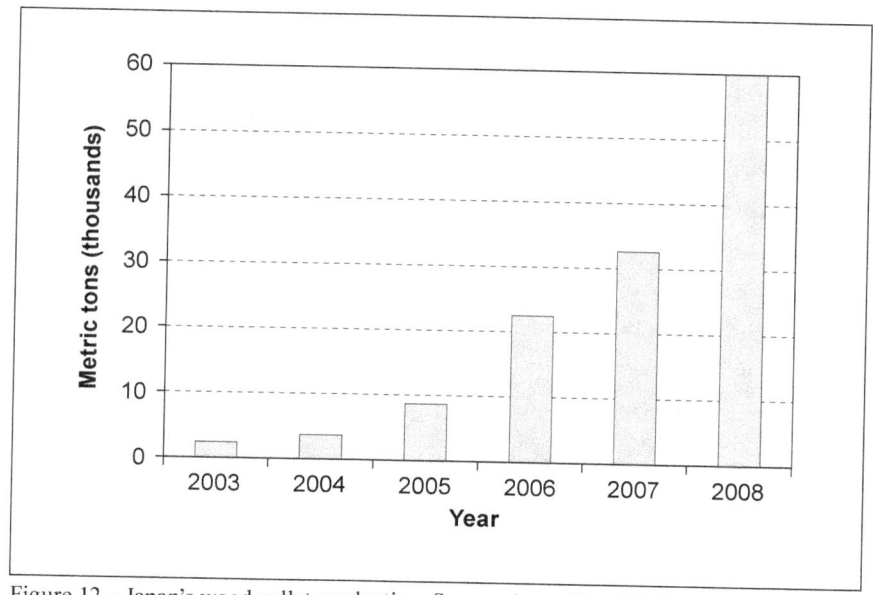

Figure 12—Japan's wood pellet production. Source: Japan Wood Pellet Association 2010.

In addition to domestic production, Japan imported approximately 49 000 metric tons of wood pellets in 2009 (Murray 2010). A majority of the imported wood pellets are sourced from Canada. Additionally, the Port of Prince Rupert has exported 120 723 metric tons of wood pellets to Asia as of August 2010, is a 36 percent increase from the same time the previous year (Port of Prince Rupert 2010).

A large portion of Japan's wood pellets are being used for electric power generation. Kansai Electric Power Corporation, a leader in this field, started using wood pellets for co-firing with coal at its Maizuru power plant in August 2008. The wood pellets will furnish approximately 120 million kilowatt hours of electricity per year, which is about 2 percent of the Maizuru plant's total output (Canada Trade Commission 2008). Another company investing heavily in wood pellets is Mitsubishi Corporation, which has acquired 45 percent of Vis Nova Trading GmbH. This German company is a global leader in Europe's wood pellet industry (Guizot 2010).

In spite of the current economic downturn, Japan still has one of the strongest economies in the world and as a signatory member of the Kyoto Protocol is committed to reducing GHG emissions. This commitment will continue to fuel demand for renewable energy. Although the wood pellet market is still in its infancy, it is growing, making this is a good time for North American exporters to explore the market and begin establishing relationships.

Conclusions

U.S. President Obama has pledged to double exports from the current level of approximately $1 trillion to $2 trillion by 2015. The center of this plan is to create a trade cabinet post that is focused on finding global markets for U.S. exports. Wood pellets fit in well with this strategy, because all three Asian nations discussed in this report have government policies that are encouraging power utilities to increase their use of renewable energy. Using wood pellets is advantageous to using other renewable energy sources such as wind, solar, and geothermal energy because it can be used with existing infrastructure for co-firing at coal-fired power plants.

Of the three markets, China has the potential to become the largest wood pellet market in Asia. Its economy is strong, energy demand is growing, and the Chinese government is looking for solutions to substitute renewable energy for coal. Additionally, the Chinese currency has appreciated against the U.S. dollar, making U.S. wood pellets easier to sell in the Chinese market. However, China imports only a very small quantity of wood pellets from North America, so this market would require substantial market development. A majority of China's wood pellet demand comes from the industrial energy market, thus market development efforts should be targeted toward government energy officials and coal-fired power plants.

The South Korean economy has weathered the global economic crisis and is now on a path to economic growth. This growth should fuel demand for wood pellets as South Korea strives to meet its goal of increasing its percentage of renewable energy to 11 percent by 2020. However, the quantity of wood pellet imports is still fairly small. Furthermore, South Korea appears to be pursuing a wood pellet strategy of joint development with other Asian countries. Overall, wood pellet demand will increase in South Korea, but it is difficult to predict what portion will be imported from North America.

As in China, a majority of Japan's wood pellet demand comes from the industrial energy sector. The leader in Japan for using wood pellets for co-firing is Kansai Electric Power Corporation. Because Japanese power utilities are held to Kyoto Protocol emission-reduction standards, there is a strong possibility that other electric utilities will follow Kansai Electric's lead and use more wood pellets as a substitute for coal.

The wood pellets markets in all three Asian countries examined are in their early stages but are growing. The primary use for wood pellets in Asia is for co-firing at coal power plants. Therefore, business development strategies should include developing relationships with coal power plants that have an interest in increasing their renewable energy output. This could be done in cooperation with the U.S. Commercial Service (app.), which assists U.S. exporters with finding customers in foreign countries and has offices in China, Japan, and South Korea. In summary, Asian government policies requiring increased use of renewable energy should stimulate demand for wood pellets, offering an opportunity for U.S. wood pellet manufacturers.

Acknowledgments

This work is based upon work supported by the U.S. Forest Service and the University of Washington. Any opinions, findings, conclusions, or recommendations expressed in this publication are those of the authors and do not necessarily reflect the views of the U.S. Department of Agriculture.

English Equivalents

When you know:	Multiply by:	To find:
Kilograms	2.205	Pounds
Metric tons or tonnes	1.102	Tons or short tons
British thermal units (BTU)	1,050	Joules (J)
Hectares	.405	Acres

Literature Cited

Bloomberg. 2010a. Wood pellet production to rise by multiples through 2020, lobby group says. http://www.bloomberg.com/news/2010-06-30/wood-pellet-production-to-rise-by-multiples-through-2020-lobby-group-says.html. June 30 (August 19, 2010).

Bloomberg. 2010b. Yuan forwards gain as U.S. steps up pressure; repo rates jump. http://www.bloomberg.com/news/2010-06-11/yuan-forwards-advance-as-u-s-congress-steps-up pressure-for-appreciation.html. June 11. (June 24, 2010).

Bloomberg. 2010c. South Korea credit ratings upgraded by Moody's to A1. http://www.bloomberg.com/apps/news?pid=20601080&sid=aeyLFBEGe9SA. April 14. (June 10, 2010).

Bloomberg. 2010d. Kan's gambit asks Japan to consider higher taxes as Upper-House vote nears. http://www.bloomberg.com/news/2010-07-05/kan-s-gambit-asks-japan-to-consider-higher-taxes-as-upper-house-vote-nears.html. July 5. (July 6, 2010).

Brackley, A.M.; Parrent, D.J. 2011. Production of wood pellets from Alaska-grown white spruce and hemlock. Gen. Tech. Rep. PNW-GTR-845. Portland, OR: U.S. Department of Agriculture, Forest Service, Pacific Northwest Research Station. 29 p.

China Daily. 2009. China plans for renewable energy. http://www.chinadaily.com.cn/bizchina/2009-08/25/content_8611790.htm. (June 28, 2010).

Canada Trade Commission. 2008. Japanese power company to start using Canadian wood pellets. May 26. http://www.tradecommissioner.gc.ca/eng/document.jsp?did=82893&cid=515&oid=146. (July 9, 2010).

Database of State Incentives for Renewables and Efficiency [DSIRE]. 2010. Renewable electricity tax credit summary. http://www.dsireusa.org/incentives/incentive.cfm?Incentive_Code=US13F. (August 3, 2010).

Energy Information Administration [EIA]. 2010. Compilation of international energy statistics. http://www.eia.doe.gov/country/country_energy_data.cfm?fips=CH. 2010 Release. (June 8, 2010).

Environmental Protection Agency [EPA]. 2009. EPA: greenhouse gases threaten public health and the environment/science overwhelmingly shows greenhouse gas concentrations at unprecedented levels due to human activity. News Release. 07 December. http://yosemite.epa.gov/opa/admpress.nsf. (April 2010).

Economist Intelligence Unit [EIU]. 2009. China country profile. London, U.K. July. 24 p.

Economist Intelligence Unit [EIU]. 2008. South Korea country profile. London, U.K. July. 19 p.

Economist Intelligence Unit [EIU]. 2010. Country GDP reports. London, U.K. July. [Pages unknown]

Food and Agriculture Organization of the United Nations [FAO]. 2010. FAOStat—global forestry statistics database. Rome, Italy. http://faostat.fao.org/site/630/default.aspx. (July 21, 2010).

Global Trade Atlas. 2010. World Trade Database. Columbia, SC. http://www.gtis.com/. (June 15, 2010).

Guizot, M. 2010. Emerging pellet markets—country profiles from around the globe. Proceedings from Pellets 2010 Conference. Stockholm, Sweden. February 2–3.

Han, G.S. 2009. Wood pellet production and trade in South Korea. Korea Association of Pellet Fuel. Cheongju, South Korea: Chungbuk National University. IEA bioenergy conference presentation. Tsukuba, Japan, October 28–30.

Hansen, M.T.; Jein, A.R.; Hayes, S.; Bateman, P. 2009. English handbook for wood pellet combustion. Milton Keynes, United Kingdom: National Energy Foundation. E.U. Intelligent Energy and Force Technology, Copenhagen, Denmark. 85 p.

International Energy Agency [IEA]. 2007. Global wood pellets markets and industry: policy drivers, market status and raw material potential. IEA Bioenergy Task 40. November.

International Energy Agency [IEA]. 2008. Korea goes for green growth. http://www.iea.org/papers/roundtable_slt/korea_oct08.pdf. September 11, 2008. (June 10, 2010).

Japan Wood Pellet Association. 2010. Japan wood pellet production statistics. http://www.mokushin.com/jpa/news/news_02.html. (July 9, 2010).

Korea Forest Service. 2010. Annual forestry statistical yearbook. Seoul, Korea.

Murray, G. 2010. Estimated global wood pellet production 2009. Prince George, BC: Wood Pellet Association of Canada.

National Development and Reform Commission. 2009. China's position on the Copenhagen Climate Change Conference. May 20. http://en.ndrc.gov.cn/newsrelease/t20090521_280382.htm. (June 28, 2010).

Nicholls, D.L. 2009. Wood energy in Alaska—case study evaluations of selected facilities. Gen. Tech. Rep. PNW-GTR-793. Portland, OR: U.S. Department of Agriculture, Forest Service, Pacific Northwest Research Station. 33 p.

Nicholls, D.L.; Crimp, P.M. 2002. Feasibility of using wood wastes to meet local heating requirements of communities in the Kenai Peninsula in Alaska. Gen. Tech. Rep. PNW-GTR-533. Portland, OR: U.S. Department of Agriculture, Forest Service, Pacific Northwest Research Station. 17 p.

Peksa-Blanchard, M.; Dolzan, P.; Grassi, A.; Heinimo, J.; Junginger, M.; Ranta, T.; Walter, A. 2007. Global wood pellets markets and industry: policy drivers, market status, and raw material potential. Task report 40. Paris, France: IEA Bioenergy.

Pellet Fuels Institute [PFI]. 2010. PFI standard specification for residential/commercial densified fuel. http://pelletheat.org/wp-content/uploads/2010/08/Draft-PFI-StandardSpecification-for-Residential-Commercial-Densified-Fuel-Revised-June-23-2010.pdf. (October 25, 2010). Superseded by http://pelletheat.org/wp-content/i[;pads/2010/01/PFI-Standard-Specification-for-Residential-Commercial-Densified-Fuel-10-25-10.pdf. (November 2010). Copies of the October 25, 2010, version are on file with: Alaska Wood Utilization and Research Center, 204 Siginaka Way, Sitka, AK 99835.

Prince Rupert Port Authority. 2010. Port of Prince Rupert May traffic summary. http://www.rupertport.com/pdf/quarterly_reports/monthly_teu_cargo_summary_july2010.pdf. (August 17, 2010).

Pew Center for Global Climate Change. 2009. Climate TechBook—Biopower Fact Book. http://www.pewclimate.org/technology/factsheet/Biopower. (June 21, 2010).

Schaub, M. 2010. Renewable energy law in China. King and Wood PRC Lawyers. Shanghai, China. June 22. http://www.kingandwood.com/lawyer.aspx?id=mark-schaub&language=en. (July 1, 2010).

Spelter, H.; Toth. T. 2008. North America's wood pellet sector. Res. Rep. FPL-RP-656. Madison, WI: U.S. Department of Agriculture, Forest Service, Forest Products Laboratory. 21 p.

Swaan, J. 2008. European wood pellet import market. Pellet Fuels Institute annual conference, Hilton Head, SC. Arlington, VA: Pellet Fuels Institute.

Thai Indian News. 2009. South Korea to produce wood pellet fuel in Indonesia. March 8. http://www.thaindian.com/newsportal/business/south-korea-to-produce-wood-pellet-fuel-in-indonesia_100164171.html. (June 15, 2010).

United Nations Statistics Division. 2010. Environmental indicators: GHGs. http://unstats.un.org/unsd/ENVIRONMENT/air_greenhouse_emissions.htm. (June 1, 2010).

United Nations Framework Convention on Climate Change [UNFCCC]. 2010. Copenhagen Accord draft. 6 p. http://unfccc.int/files/meetings/cop_15/application/pdf/cop15_cph_auv.pdf. (April 2010).

Wang, C.; Jinyue, Y. 2005. Feasibility analysis of wood pellets production and utilization in China as a substitute for coal. International Journal of Green Energy. 2(1): 91–107.

World Bank. 2010. Global outlook summary 2008–2012. http://web.worldbank.org/external/default/main?theSitePK=659149&pagePK=2470434&contentMDK=20370107&menuPK=659160&piPK=2470429. (June 18, 2010).

Yamamoto, K.; Wang, Z.; Liu, A. 2008. Increasing production of wood pellets in China. Biomass-Asia workshop. Guangzhou, China. December 4–6.

Appendix: Sources for Wood Pellet and Export Assistance

American Chamber of Commerce in Japan
Masonic 39 MT Bldg. 10F
2-4-5 Azabudai, Minato-Ku
Tokyo 106-0041, Japan
Phone: (81) 3-3433-5381
Fax: (81) 3-3433-8454
http://www.accj.or.jp
E-Mail: programs@accj.or.jp

American Hardwood Export Council
U.S. Embassy 10F, 2-11-5
Nishi-Temma, Kita-ku,
Osaka 530-0047, Japan
Phone: (81) 6-6315-5101
Fax: (81) 6-6315-5103
E-mail: info@ahec-japan.org
http://www.ahec.org/

American Softwoods China Office
Room 4706, Tower 1 Grand Gateway
1 Hangqiao Road,
Shanghai 200030, China
Phone: (86) 21-6448-4401
Fax: (86) 21-6448-4404
http://www.afandpa-china.org/

Chinese Ministries and Councils Web Site
http://english.gov.cn/

European Biomass Industry Organization
http://www.eubia.org/

Export.gov
A list of export resources offered by the U.S. government.
http://www.export.gov/

Japan Coal Energy Center
9F, Meiji Yasuda Seimei Mita Bldg.
3-14-10 Mita, Minato-ku
Tokyo 108-0073, Japan
Phone: (81) 3-6400-5191
Fax: (81)-3-3-6400-5206
E-mail: jcoal-qa@jcoal.or.jp
http://www.jcoal.or.jp/

Japan External Trade Association
(San Francisco Office)
235 Pine Street, Suite 1700
San Francisco CA 94104
Phone: (415) 392-1333
Fax: (415) 788-6927

Japan Wood Pellet Association
Minato-Ku Akasaka 2-2-19
Tokyo 107-0052, Japan
Phone: 03-3585-5595
Fax: 03-3585-5598
http://www.mokushin.com/jpa/index2.html

Korea Chamber of Commerce and Industry
45 4ga Namdaemunro, Jung-gu
Seoul 100-743, Korea
Phone: (82) 2-6050-3114
Fax: (82) 2-6050-3400
http://english.korcham.net/

Pellet Fuels Institute
1901N Moore St Suite 600
Arlington, VA 22209
Phone: (703) 522-6778
http://www.pelletheat.org/

Softwoods Export Council, Japan Office
AIOS Toranomon 9F
1-6-12 Nishi Shinbashi, Minato-ku,
Tokyo 105-0003, Japan,
Phone: (03) 3501-2131

South Korea Energy Department, Ministry of Knowledge Economy
88 Gwanmoonro, Gwacheon-si, Gyeonggi-do,
Seoul 427-723, Korea
Phone: (81) 2-1577-0900
http://www.mke.go.kr/language/eng/policy/Epolicies.jsp

The U.S./China Business Council
U.S. Office
1818 N Street, NW, Suite 200
Washington, DC 20036
Phone: (202) 429-0340
Beijing Office
CITIC Building, Suite 10-01
19 Jianguomenwai Dajie
Beijing 100004, China
Phone: (86) 10-6592-0727
http://www.uschina.org/

U.S.-China Chamber of Commerce
2309 Portman Center, 52 Caihong North Road,
Ningbo, Zhejiang Province, China 315040
Phone: (86) 574-8795-3268
Fax: (86) 574-879-53267
E-mail: jianmingzhang@usccc.org
http://www.usccc.org/

U.S. Commercial Service, China
Cathy Wang, Commercial Specialist
Phone: (86) 20 8667-4011 ext.616
Fax: (86) 20 8666-6409
E-mail: Cathy.Wang@trade.gov
http://www.buyusa.gov/china/en/

U.S. Commercial Service in China
U.S. Embassy Beijing
No. 55 An Jia Lou Road,
Chaoyang District
Beijing 100600, China
Phone: (86-10) 8531-3000
Fax: (86-10) 8531-3701
E-mail: Office.Beijing@trade.gov
http://www.buyusa.gov/china/en/

U.S. Commercial Service, Japan
Kazuhisa Takabatake, Senior Commercial Specialist
Phone: (81) 6-6315-5955
Fax: (81) 6-6315-5963
E-mail: Kazuhisa.Takabatake@trade.gov
http://www.buyusa.gov/japan/en/

U.S. Commercial Service, South Korea
Nathan Huh, Commercial Specialist
Phone: (82) 2-397-4535
Fax: (82) 2-739-1628
E-mail: Nathan.Huh@trade.gov
http://www.buyusa.gov/korea/en/

Wood Pellet Association of Canada
P.O. Box 2989
1877 Upper McKinnon Road
Revelstoke, BC V0E 2S0, Canada
Phone: (250) 837-8821
http://www.pellet.org/

Wood Pellet Fuel Association
42 Prospect St. Whitefield, NH 03598
Phone: (603) 837-9759
http://www.woodpelletfuel.org/